Mali

A Prospect of Peace?

Contents

front cover: James Hawkins/Oxfam

Jeremy Hartley/Oxfam

Oxfam UK and Ireland   **Rhéal Drisdelle**

This book converted to digital file in 2010

Jeremy Hartley/Oxfam

clockwise from top left

Tonka market, near Goundam

Touareg boys taking water from a well in Essuk village, near Kidal, Gao

River Niger at Bourem

Pounding grain in Dili village, north-west Mali

Bali village, north-west Mali

Mike Goldwater/Oxfam

left On the road from Mopti to Goundam

❛ *The situation is very difficult and very fragile. But I have never felt so sure that we have the means to resolve our problems, and that Mali holds the key to its own future. We are not asking the international community for help to walk, only to stand up: we can do the walking ourselves.* ❜

President Alpha Oumar Konaré, May 1995

Jeremy Hartley/Oxfam

above Touareg and Bella men gather to work on a rainwater-catchment scheme near Timbuktu

right A map of West Africa

A land of paradoxes

In purely statistical terms, it is hard to present a positive picture of Mali. This country of over ten million people — expected to have increased to 24 million by the year 2025 — is a world leader in several categories: highest infant mortality rates, highest maternal mortality rates, highest fertility rates, and highest illiteracy rates.

Mali is one of the largest countries in West Africa, five times the size of the United Kingdom. It is a country of paradoxes. Considered one of the five poorest countries in the world, it nevertheless contains some of the richest gold deposits in all of Africa. Its soils are believed to be rich in minerals, such as manganese, lithium, iron, and diamonds. Yet, because of the country's size and lack of infrastructure, such as roads and communications systems, exploration of these resources has hardly begun. Much of the land-mass of Mali — roughly two thirds — is either dry, hot, and windswept Saharan sand, or arid and severely depleted Sahelian soil. In spite of these unfavourable conditions, Mali is the second-biggest producer of cotton in Africa. It also grows enough rice and cereals to feed its own people, and a surplus to export to its neighbours.

Mali is a country of farmers, herders, and fishing communities; yet its main export to the world has always been Malians themselves. Most Malians are traders to the core, and will trade anything with anyone; but Mali does not manufacture anything much, and has to rely on imports for most of its consumer goods.

Malians are essentially a rural people. Four out of five live in the countryside; but young people in search of a living are

above Bananas for sale in a Bamako market

James Hawkins/Oxfam

5

flocking to the cities, where disease, hunger, and misery await them. This is a country where tradition rules, where male elders dominate and define the world; but as more and more young people seek work in the cities and in countries near and far, they encounter a more modern version of reality, and gaps are opening up in the traditional way of life. Women's lives are beginning to change in a society where they are still denied a voice, yet contribute most to the survival of their communities when the men are obliged to leave home to find work and money.

below A Touareg girl in Gao

Jeremy Hartley/Oxfam

Mali is one of the oldest Islamic nations in sub-Saharan Africa, but it has evolved its own distinctively relaxed form of Islam, while remaining very close to the animistic and traditional beliefs of earlier times. Fundamentalism might be expected to thrive in a context of severe economic hardship and culture clashes between the generations, but Malians remain wary of extremism in both religion and politics.

A mosaic of people

From north to south, a combination of climate, genes, ancestry, and history has forged several distinct cultural groups. In the Saharan sands and rocky terrain of the far north live the Tamasheq or Touareg people. Of Berber origin, with nomadic ways and light-coloured skin, they live on the `fault line' between the Arab world of the north and the black African world of the south. Northern Mali also has a small population of Arab ancestry and Moorish culture who mainly live in or near Timbuktu; their origins are nomadic, but many in recent years have become traders and boutique owners in the cities.

Farmers, herders, and fishermen

Co-existing with these lighter-skinned nomads are the Songhay, who are mainly farmers. They are the majority population in these northern expanses, but live mostly in the towns along the banks of the Niger River from Timbuktu to Gao. Although they constitute only about one tenth of the total population of Mali, they are highly influential people: with an unusually high level of education, many occupy important posts in the army, the civil service, and the political world.

The Peuhl or Fulani herders are found everywhere in Mali where large herds of cattle, sheep, and goats are grazed. Formerly a nomadic people (Fulani can be found throughout West Africa), the Peuhl in Mali have for the most part settled down.

Mike Goldwater/Oxfam

right A young girl in Damba village, north-west Mali

Jeremy Hartley/Oxfam

above A Touareg man in Gangano village, near Bourem

left A boy with a goat in Djenne, central Mali

Catherine Howe/Oxfam

On the Niger River, from Bamako to Gao, Bozo fishermen can be seen with their families, following the fish along the length of the river. Some still practise collective fishing, with nets that can measure more than 300 metres. Depending on the season and the type of fishing, the men may choose to leave their families behind or to bring them along. Women play an important part in marketing the fish, which in most cases is smoked.

The Dogon people

In north central Mali, along the Bandiagara Cliffs, between the Niger River and the border with Burkina Faso, live the Dogon people. These hardy and courageous communities live literally on the edge of survival. The Dogon Plateau, a land of strange rock formations and steep cliffs, is a harsh and arid environment. There are three groups of Dogon: those living on the Plateau; those who have had to move on to the plain in order to survive; and those still clinging to life on the cliffs.

The Bandiagara Cliffs run north to south for over 200 km and vary in height from 300 to 500 metres. Many Dogon living along the cliffs climb up and down the vertiginous ridges several times a day, the women often laden with children and balancing 20-litre jugs on their heads. Produce is lowered up and down the cliffs with the help of rope made from the bark of baobab trees.

Dogon culture, with its own alphabet, its five-day week, and references to stellar bodies only recently identified by Western scientists, has been the focus of numerous documentaries and anthropological studies. It has been kept alive by its isolation from all external influences; but, threatened with extermination by droughts and the degradation of their

below The Bandiagara Cliffs, home of the Dogon people. Caves in the cliff have been used for centuries as tombs for the dead.

environment, the Dogons are now obliged to open themselves to the outside world, and they risk losing their unique identity. Much of their culture is rooted in reverence for their ancestors, who are celebrated with sacred masks in rituals such as the *sigui*, which is held once every 60 years. The oldest man in the community is 'retired' from the village to live in a nearby cave, where he is venerated and fed by the community and, according to Dogon belief, washed by a serpent which appears every night. The riches of the Dogon culture are in stark contrast to the barren environment in which they live.

People of the south

Southern Mali is dominated by the culture of the Bambara people, who comprise about one third of the total population. Bambara is the main commercial language, spoken by most other ethnic groups and used throughout the country. The Bambara people are to be found all over Mali, but most are concentrated in the region of Ségou, where they make a living from growing cotton and cereals.

The Malinke people live in the southern-most part of Mali, as well as in northern Guinea. Famed hunters and warriors, the Malinke converted to Islam only in the twentieth century. Their traditional hunters' societies, with secret initiation rites, still thrive to this day.

The Sarakole live mostly in the western-most area, in the Kayes region on the borders with Senegal, Guinea, and Mauritania. Renowned for their trading skills, many Sarakole have had to leave this isolated region after the disastrous droughts of the last twenty years. Many have emigrated to France, where they manage to eke out a living in difficult conditions doing menial jobs, but somehow contriving to send much-needed cash to their families back home. While some have succeeded in obtaining French citizenship and bringing their families to join them, most are only tolerated by the French authorities, and it is a common sight on Air France flights from Paris to Bamako to see manacled Sarakole men being escorted to their seats by French *gendarmes*. Those who are allowed to remain in France and elsewhere have created dynamic associations which now channel their meagre savings to be invested in community-development initiatives at home.

Le cousinage

Like many African countries, Mali is a compound of widely differing ethnic groups; but Malians have learned to live together, sharing scarce resources and respecting each other's traditions. One reason is that they have developed a unique system of social interchange, which is called *cousinage*.

Cousinage implies, in theory if not in fact, that most Malians are related, despite the existence of more than a dozen major cultural groups. For more than 900 years, empires have come and gone; people from different ethnic groups have inter-married; former slaves and former slave owners have become intrinsically linked with one another. (Because of the vagaries of history, the same group could very well have been both masters and serfs at various times.)

Examples of *cousinage* are encountered daily. No Malian will greet another without enquiring about his or her family name, ancestral origins, and geographical provenance. Once this is settled, there follows what sounds to uninitiated ears like a series of insults: A accuses B of being nothing but a descendant of slaves; of being stupid and ignorant on account of his or her family trade; of being bone-idle because he or she comes from this or that region ... and so on. In reply, B might claim that, without his or her group's input into the economy, A and A's family — and indeed society in general — would not be able to survive.

All this is not just a social convention. It is safety valve for the release of pressure. If, for example, a person is involved in a traffic accident (an all too common event in downtown Bamako), having made sure that no one is seriously injured, one party will blame the accident on the fact that the other belongs to such and such an ethnic group and is therefore an imbecile. After a short but heated argument, one of the two will offer to accompany the other to the hospital, or to have the vehicle towed away.

Cousinage exists not only between ethnic groups, but between different castes within each cultural grouping. As such, if one's family name is Diabate, one is regarded as a *griot*, even if one is unable to sing the praises of others, as *griots* are expected to do. Equally, a Thiam will be considered a blacksmith, even though he has a PhD degree from the University of Oxford.

At a time when 'ethnic cleansing' and genocide are depressingly prevalent around the world, *cousinage* is an invaluable means of defusing potential conflicts. The disadvantage of the system is that people seem to be eternally identified with and confined to one particular group or livelihood. While it may not do wonders for social mobility, Mali's deep-rooted concern with its past partly explains why it has not become dragged into ethnic blood-letting of the kind we have seen in Rwanda and Former Yugoslavia. Tensions and uncertainties do exist in Mali, as we shall see; but *cousinage* permits hard truths to be aired and certain intermediaries to intervene, where antagonistic ethnic groups might elsewhere resort to violence.

'I grew up not seeing any difference between Songhay and Touareg. There is an affectionate term in the Songhay language which loosely means "Our Touareg". My family had many Touareg friends, who often came to the house and stayed in our compound for several days. They were like part of our family. Whenever they came they would bring gifts, things like butter, or dried meat, or cheese; and when they left, they'd take tea or other gifts from us. So there was a sort of communion between the two communities.'

(Sada Maiga, a field worker with an international agency)

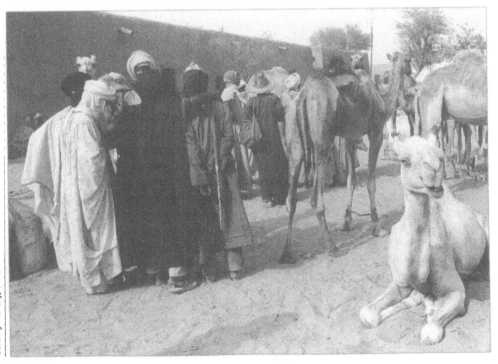

Jeremy Hartley/Oxfam

left No Malian will greet another without enquiring about his or her family name, ancestral origins, and geographical provenance.

Culture old and new

The music of Mali

The power of the past in Mali is well illustrated by the survival of the *griot* tradition. *Griots* are living institutions, a legacy from the days when oral historians recounted the past glories of the group, and sang the praises of the rich and powerful. They belong to a caste system: you are born a *griot* if you belong to a certain lineage. Although story-tellers and praise-singers are present almost everywhere in west and central Africa, few would dispute the claim of Mali to be the *griot* capital of the continent.

Still today, no social function like a wedding or a naming ceremony takes place without at least one *griot* present to sing the praises of the family and the guests. TV and radio programmes are dominated by the latest recordings of over 200 professional *griots* (and *griotes*, as this is one of the few occupations open to both women and men in Mali).

But, as with many other customs, modern life and growing impoverishment have diminished this once proud and socially useful role of story-teller and praise-singer. Nowadays, *griots* are becoming the musical equivalent of beggars: anyone will sing the praises of anyone, if there is money to be made from it.

Yet the tradition persists, and along the way some remarkable singers have been elevated from the status of local *griot* to international fame, singing love songs and other traditional melodies. Singers like Ami Koita and Oumou Sangaré have performed in London, Paris, and New York, and their recordings may be bought almost anywhere in the world.

above Typical Dogon carving in the traditional style used to decorate granary doors

James Hawkins/Oxfam

above 'Monsieur Taptap', a blanket seller in Mopti

Couture, literature, and cinema

On another international stage, Chris Seydou, the great Malian designer and stylist, worked in the fashion trade in Paris and New York for several years, before returning to Mali in the late 1980s to revive a cloth-dyeing technique as old as Malian culture itself. The tradition of *bogolan* was almost forgotten before Chris Seydou rescued and rejuvenated it. He died in 1993 at the age of 44. His legacy has been to rekindle interest in the tradition, and to encourage young Malian designers and tailors to renew their links with their past.

Mali has produced many writers, historians, and poets, among them the great Amadou Hampaté Ba, 'the wise man of Bandiagara'. Of Peuhl origin, he was brought up during the French colonial era; as a young boy he worked as a translator for the French administrators. He collected traditional tales and legends during his travels — he once walked the length and breadth of West Africa — and combined this with his self-taught knowledge and acquired wisdom to compile a most amazing series of books of historical fiction, philosophical thoughts, and Peuhl initiation rites. Amadou Hampaté Ba died in 1992 at the age of 91.

Equally, Malians have excelled in the twentieth-century craft of cinema. Cheik Oumar Sissoko and Soulemane Cisse, to mention only two, have written and directed some notable films, surviving as film craftsmen in a poor country through the sheer power of their cinematic vision. Their films tell stories and denounce injustices and poverty, and have won awards in most of the international film festivals, including Cannes, where *Yeelen* was the first African film ever to do so.

Everyday culture

Malian culture is not the preserve of a celebrated few. It is as rich, varied, and complex as the nation's geography,

Another performer and singer who has won international fame is Salif Keita. Although not of *griot* stock, this Malinke singer has a unique and powerful voice. He has surmounted prejudice against his albino colouring to win the hearts of Malians with his lyrical poetry, mostly taken from traditional tales and legends. Based in Paris for several years, he has toured the world and shared the stage with the best and brightest in show business.

At the 1994 Grammy Awards ceremony, Ali Farka Touré became the first African to win this coveted music prize, given by his peers for his outstanding abilities as one of the greatest living blues guitarists. Born in the Timbuktu area, he has lived in New York and Los Angeles for over 20 years, though he keeps in close contact with his home country and can be seen regularly in clubs and jam sessions in any large Malian city.

history, and ethnic groups. Most Malian men and women dress in the traditional *boubou*: a richly coloured, flowing gown which adds elegance, vitality, and decorum to any village or city market. Especially on civic and religious holidays, this flamboyant garment is a sight to marvel at.

Every day, tea-drinking groups called *grins* meet to take part in the ceremony of the three teas. (*'The first cup is strong like life; the second is sweet like love; and the third is bitter, like death.'*) They discuss the latest news in politics or sports, and the juiciest gossip in the neighbourhood.

Malian cuisine may vary from region to region, but does not offer a great deal of choice. Most southerners will share a common meal of *tô*, a pudding made from pounded millet, served with a sauce of meat and okra. Also popular is *bassi*, a couscous made from millet, served with sauces made of baobab leaves and a kind of spinach. In the north, the cuisine of the Songhay and Touareg features thick, doughy pancakes, also served with wild leaves. But no meal anywhere in Mali is complete without meat, poultry, or fish: vegetarianism is almost unknown.

In towns and villages throughout the country, traditional ceremonies, dances, and festivities still mark the passing of the seasons and the major events of life. In the initiation rites of the secret Malinke hunters' societies, the movements of the Dogon stalk dancers, and the slow rhythmic grace of the Songhay *takumba* dance, Malians continue to celebrate their distinctive cultural heritage.

right A traditional Dogon mask

James Hawkins/Oxfam

below A map of Mali, showing places mentioned in this book

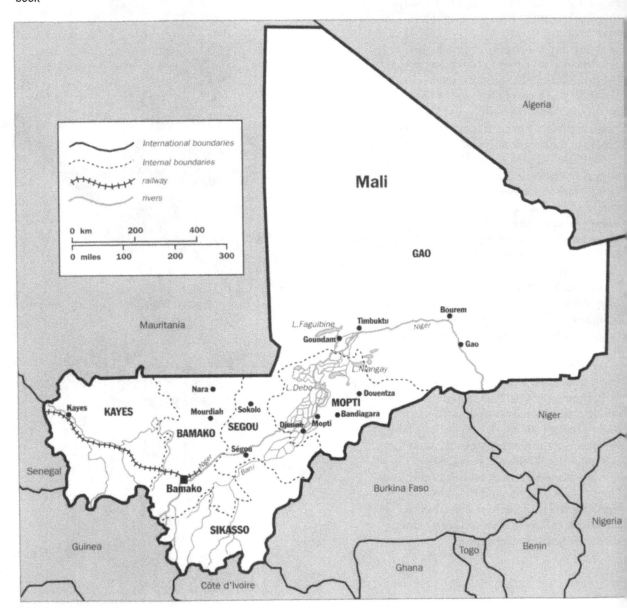

Timbuktu and the empires

Jeremy Hartley/Oxfam

above A camel train in Goundam

Few people outside Africa can readily locate Mali on a world map, but most would recognise the name Timbuktu. This ancient Saharan city was once the centre of a powerful empire, one in a succession which ruled much of West Africa for many centuries. It is another paradox that prosperous empires flourished throughout most of the last thousand years in what is now one of the poorest regions of the world.

Yet the prosperity of former Malian empires is no accident of history. Although the country is totally landlocked, it contains three important waterways: the Niger, which flows from the Guinean Mountains across all of western Africa; the Senegal, which opens on to the Atlantic Ocean; and the Bani, which weaves through southern Mali to merge with the Niger to constitute the rich Niger Delta. To the north of these rivers there is the Sahara Desert, which brought wealth to Mali in its position at the cross-roads of trans-Saharan trade.

From the rich soils of the river beds, the southern, sedentary, and negroid Malians exchanged crops and gold with the nomadic, light-skinned Berbers from the north, who brought salt and other exotic goods from the wider Arabic and Mediterranean worlds. The ancient interdependence between north and south has produced a unique culture, rooted in tradition and respect of differences, bound together by ethnic mingling and inter-marriage, united by the Islamic faith while yet keeping ancestral animistic beliefs alive.

A succession of empires

Islam arrived early in Mali, through the *jihad* which conquered north Africa following the death of the Prophet Mohammed in the seventh century AD. But its influence was confined to the north of the Niger River, mainly among the Berber (Touareg) and Arab (Moor) populations. Some historians regard the arrival of Islam as a factor in the creation of cities, but the truth is that urban centres like Djenne, on the Niger River, had

existed in southern Mali as early as the third century BC.

The Malinke Empire

History and myth meet with the creation of the first Malian Empire under the legendary Sundyata Keita, whose rags-to-riches story is still part of oral tradition throughout the Sahel. His empire created much of the social organisation which remains very much alive to this day. Influential from the thirteenth to the fifteenth century, it reached its pinnacle during the reign of Mansa Moussa (1312-1337), whose pilgrimage to Mecca, taking with him eight tons of gold, depressed the price of gold in Mecca and Cairo for many years. It is generally believed that two thirds of the world's gold stock was then in the hands of this Malinke empire.

below The spectacular mosque in Mopti, built of mud-bricks

left A Fulani nomad herding goats beside a field of maize

The Songhay Empire

However, by the fifteenth century, attacks by neighbours and the discontent of peripheral groups brought the end of Malinke power and the birth of the Songhay Empire, created by Askia Mohammed on the edge of the Sahara and the Niger River in northern Mali. At height of the Sonrhoys' imperial power around 1550, Gao and Timbuktu each had a population estimated at 100,000, and Timbuktu, recognised as Islam's holiest site, had become one of the leading universities in the world, with over 15,000 students. With the commercial city of Djenne to the south doing trade with Italy and England via Morocco, the Songhay Empire combined a rich intellectual life with lucrative commerce.

This golden age came to an end in 1590, when competition for control of the trans-Saharan trade routes brought an invasion from Morocco. Timbuktu was pillaged in 1594, the university was destroyed, and most of the academics were deported to Marrakesh.

The Bambara Kingdom

The remains of the empire fought for control through the next century, but it was not until 1712 that a new force emerged to consolidate power over this immense territory. The Bambara Kingdom, established by Biton Coulibaly, lasted until 1808, sharing power during most of this period with the Peuhl (Fulani) of Macina. These two powers represented the two livelihoods which, to this day, constitute the backbone of the Malian economy: farming and herding.

Divided by rival and tribal conflicts, their empires soon fell to the invading forces of El Hadj Omar Tall, leading a *jihad* from Guinea and Senegal in the mid-1800s. Still remembered to this day for its 'convert or die' ferocity, this invasion further sundered an already divided land. The sons of Omar Tall further partitioned the territory, which became too weak to resist the last invasion of all: the French incursion from deepest West Africa.

The French Empire

Europeans had explored parts of Mali as early as 1791, with the British expedition of Major Houghton, who was followed in 1795 by Mungo Park (the first European to set foot in Timbuktu); but a European military invasion was not in the making until the 1880s. For this ultimate invasion, the Malians created a last empire under Samory Touré, which at its height comprised most of present-day Mali, Guinea, and Côte d'Ivoire. This empire resisted French encroachment for a time, but the invaders finally got the better of Samory, who was arrested in 1897 and deported to Gabon, where he died in 1900. Sporadic clashes occurred until the 1920s, the last involving the indomitable Dogons.

The colonial legacy

The new French rulers incorporated their newly captured land in a territory called 'French West Africa', part of a vast conglomerate designated as 'French Sudan'. From the start, Mali was to be the bread-basket of this vast region, providing rice for French colonies along the coast, and cotton for the textile industry of France.

The French presence in Mali was marked by over-ambitious irrigation projects which used forced labour and ignored local knowledge of land use and patterns of tenure. The most famous project involved taming the annual floods of the Niger River, with works that rivalled those of the British in the Nile Basin. These works remain to this day, and the Office du Niger is the principal provider of rice for the country. In addition, the colonial power built a new capital for Mali: Bamako, which was a sleepy riverside town until their arrival.

Apart from these two singular developments, the French imperialists in Mali never achieved, or tried to achieve, the in-roads they made in countries like

below Children learning French in Kokolo Village, on the Dogon Plateau

James Hawkins/Oxfam

Côte d'Ivoire and Senegal. This landlocked territory, with its harsh climate and stubborn inhabitants, did not offer to France any interesting features other than its strategic location deep inside the continent. No major infrastructure remains from these imperial times, other than the irrigation network on the Niger and the railroad from Dakar to Bamako.

Otherwise, Malians may choose to remember the French for four reasons. First, because they destroyed traditional customs such as the *dina*, the code of conduct by which all disputes over land tenure were resolved between the pastoralists, cultivators, and fishing communities. Second, because they forcibly conscripted Malians to fight in two world wars. Third, because to this day French is the official language of the country, although it is spoken by only a tiny minority of educated urbanites and bureaucrats. And fourth, because the French destabilised the society of the nomadic Tamasheq (Touaregs) by their requisition of camel herds for the war effort in 1916. The effects of this last intervention are still being played out in Mali today.

In most of the country, during the 60 or so years of the French colonial era, for most Malians life continued as before. But with the end of French rule in 1960 and the creation of a new and independent Mali, dominated by French-trained administrators, ordinary Malians would find themselves thrust into the modern era with alien institutions bent on discarding traditional ways. The Malianised bureaucracy would relentlessly pursue the colonial objective of imposing its own rules, with the disdain for the peasant class which it had learned from the former French power. This legacy, too, had consequences that linger to this day.

The disappearance of the dina

The *dina*, instituted by Cheik Amadou, was a complex set of rules which governed livelihoods in the Niger Delta and throughout Mali. It imposed regulations and penalties to ensure the sharing of natural resources among herders, farmers, and fishing communities. A decentralised institution which empowered local chieftains and communities, it defined the routes which pastoralists and nomads should take with their herds, and set the parameters and relationships between farmland and pastures.

The disappearance of the *dina* at the hands of French and Malian administrations bent on establishing their own influence played havoc with the country's future. The droughts, environmental degradation, and demographic growth of the last 20 years have put very severe pressures on systems of land tenure and access to natural resources. The disappearance of the ways of the *dina* and the arrival of unscrupulous administrators ready to resolve land-tenure conflicts by bribery, corruption, and intimidation only intensified the depletion of resources that was already impoverishing Mali.

below Swarms of desert locusts, like the one caught here by a Malian entomologist, can devastate fields of millet and maize

Mike Goldwater/Oxfam

From hope to despair

Jeremy Hartley/Oxfam

above Countless animals died during the drought which ravaged Mali in 1984–85

Independence and after

The end of the European imperial age, following the second world war, brought calls for independence across Africa, and Malians were to play a leading role during this period. Led by the articulate panafricanist, Modibo Keita, Mali set out towards independence through a regional federation with Senegal, attained in April 1960. Unfortunately, this almost unique attempt to create a federative African structure to erase European-imposed territorial divisions did not last long, and in September of the same year the Federation of Mali split and the Republic of Mali was created.

Still led by Modibo Keita, Mali quickly chose to break its ties with France and become a socialist republic. Not wanting Mali to be perceived as a Soviet or Chinese puppet state, Modibo Keita played a key role, along with Presidents Nasser of Egypt and N'krumah of Ghana, in the creation of the Organisation of African Unity (OAU) and the setting up of a Third World forum, the Non-Aligned States.

From socialism ...

The Malian experience of socialism *à l'africaine* was to prove disastrous and played a key role in Keita's overthrow by a military coup in 1968. The centrally managed economy had replaced competitive markets with State agencies, rural co-operatives, and State enterprises. By 1967, foreign debts, depleted currency reserves, and failing agricultural production forced a devaluation of the Malian franc and a re-entry into the Franc zone. Nevertheless, those years are still

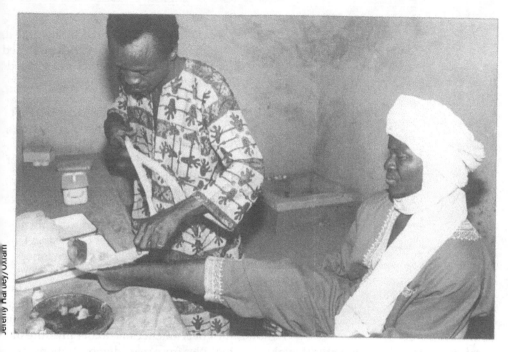

left Rural health services, neglected during the UPDM years, are now denied funding under the terms of the economic structural adjustment programme

fondly remembered by many Malians for improvements to the education and health services, and the sense of national unity which survives to this day, rekindling hope and pride. While his policies may have been rejected, Modibo Keïta remains close to the hearts of every Malian. His death in detention in the 1970s, in mysterious circumstances, only contributed to the growing disenchantment of those opposed to the rule of the military.

... through drought and dictatorship

The military coup of 1968, led by Moussa Traoré, set up a military dictatorship (1968-1974) which evolved into a one-party autocratic system, the Union Democratique du Peuple Malien (UPDM), which in all lasted for 23 years. The greatest legacy of those dark years was the institutionalising of corruption, not only as a form of government but also as a way of life. Those years were also marked by two disastrous droughts, in 1973-74 and again in 1984-85. One effect of the droughts was to open up the country to

international aid — which for the most part went into the coffers of government and party officials.

The 1970s and 1980s were difficult times for Malians in general, as the effects of the droughts drove hundreds of thousands to Bamako and other urban centres in quest of new livelihoods. The droughts only accentuated a process of desertification, which had been triggered by a combination of poor management, inappropriate government policies, and the growing population's demand for ever-scarcer resources. Crop yields dwindled in the Sahelian regions, and the dismal economic situation was made even worse by restrictions introduced under the structural adjustment programme (SAP) launched in 1982.

... to dreams made in Washington

The structural adjustment programme was intended to streamline government bureaucracies, match national spending with national revenues, impose financial discipline, and encourage the private sector to invest and create jobs. Most observers would agree that many of these

James Hawkins/Oxfam

above *'Victory for the democratic movement. Descent into hell for the bloodstained and corrupt regime of Moussa and his clan'* — press coverage of the events of 23–26 March 1991

reforms were needed, but little thought was given to the social costs that would have to be paid. The adjustment programme created unemployment and further weakened the education and health services, hitting the poorest and most vulnerable particularly hard. The role of the State was weakened, but very little else was offered to fill the void.

The statistics speak for themselves: in the early 1990s, UN indicators placed Mali among the five poorest nations in the world; annual per capita income was estimated at $270 and life expectancy at 45 years; health services reached a bare 15 per cent of the population; enrolment in primary education was at an all-time low of 23 per cent; and literacy among adults was estimated at 16 per cent.

To compound these problems, people living in rural areas (about 80 per cent of the population living) were finding it harder and harder to farm smaller and smaller plots, as population growth outpaced productive resources. Livestock used to be Mali's main export, but pastoral areas continued to shrink as desertification increased, and nomadic herders were hard-pressed to sustain a

precarious existence. In this bleak context, the nomadic Touaregs launched an armed rebellion against the corrupt and divided Traoré regime in June 1990.

... and the downfall of the UDPM

Discontent was also growing in the cities, where the young educated elite, sacked from government jobs under the terms of the SAP, were becoming 'the new poor'. Inspired by democratic movements spreading throughout Africa, civil associations began to emerge in Mali, armed with independent newspapers, demanding greater political freedom, multi-party politics, and full civil rights.

With the Touaregs in open revolt in the north, and the army unable to defeat their highly mobile and well-armed opponents, the government came under pressure in the cities from mass demonstrations, as the democratic movement joined forces with thousands of students protesting against the lack of investment in education.

Events culminated in the bloody weekend of 23–26 March 1991, when hundreds of people, men and women, young and old, were killed and injured when troops fired on suicidal marches on the Presidential Palace. On the 26th, a group of progressive officers, led by Colonel Amadou Toumany Touré, toppled the regime and arrested Moussa Traoré and his notorious associates.

But the disastrous economic and environmental crisis briefly described above would not disappear with Traoré. In the years ahead, Mali would face enormous challenges. The very survival of this proud and ancient people depends on three quests: for democracy and decentralisation; for peace and reconciliation; and for sustainable development. These quests are inextricably interlinked; most observers agree that the third depends largely on the success or otherwise of the first two.

Democracy and decentralisation

Mali is at a crossroads in its destiny. The changes that have taken place since the tragic days of March 1991 are as astounding as they are fragile, and few observers would have dared to predict a positive outcome.

In the days after the coup, Colonel Touré, or 'ATT' as he is fondly called, named himself President of a transitional deliberative body that included representatives of each major association that had contributed to the downfall of the previous regime, including Touareg rebel leaders. For the next 14 months, the transitional government organised a national conference to debate a new social contract and draw up a constitution; set up a referendum on the proposed constitution; put in place the rules by which open, free, and multi-party elections were to be held; oversaw municipal, legislative, and presidential elections under the auspices of international observers; and signed a *Pacte National* which, in principle, ended the Touareg revolt.

The former dictator, his generals, and the principal power-barons of the one-party apparatus were prosecuted in what international observers declared to be a fair and open trial. Moussa Traoré and four of his generals were found guilty of crimes against humanity for their roles in the killing of innocent demonstrators. Sentenced to death, they remain in jail awaiting a presidential reprieve.

In an atmosphere of great expectations and remarkable social order, ATT was able to transfer power in June 1992 to the first democratically elected President of Mali: Alpha Oumar Konaré, a respected intellectual, teacher, and historian.

James Hawkins/Oxfam

An experiment in democracy

The new constitution guaranteed freedom of speech, freedom of the press, and freedom of assembly. In a few short months more than 20 newspapers were on the streets, a dozen independent radio stations were on the newly liberated airwaves, and thousands of civil associations were organised. From consumer groups to women's associations, all sought new-found freedoms after decades of silence and submission.

But the promises of instant prosperity to be ushered in by democracy soon

above Producing literacy materials in the office of Molibemo, a local non-government organisation. More than 600 NGOs have been established since 1991

collided with the harsh realities of rebuilding a country which had suffered years of neglect and corruption. President Konaré was perceived as weak and indecisive when he refused any show of force against a rising tide of demonstrations, violence, and political opportunism. Individuals, associations, political parties, and the media were inventing the rules of democracy as they went along, and at times it seemed that the new Malian democracy would be short-lived.

The first major challenge came from the students who had contributed the most to toppling the previous regime. Moussa Traoré, the former dictator, had earned their animosity by deciding, at the World Bank's insistence, to cut back spending on education. For decades the Malian education system had been in a shambles. Lack of investment, overcrowding, too few teachers, most of them poorly trained and concentrated in the cities: these were the hallmarks of the Traoré regime. Primary education in rural areas was neglected in favour of secondary and higher education in the cities; the result was enormous illiteracy rates and wasted human potential. In a mainly rural and agricultural country, the Malian education system, modelled on the French system, produced sophisticated graduates able to analyse the works of Victor Hugo, but unable to tell the difference between millet and sorghum crops.

Nevertheless, this alien system conferred one advantage on those families whose children did progress beyond primary school: bursaries for all, regardless of attainment, intended to cover the costs of living and studying away from home. In such a poor country with large families and few jobs, the bursary (a legacy of the socialist era) became an important addition to the monthly family revenue.

The new government, under pressure from the World Bank and most of its foreign donors, could no longer pay the bursaries. The student movement, which had given hundreds of lives to the cause of democracy, was now being required by the newly elected democratic government to make more sacrifices. The clash that ensued was to shake loose the very foundations of the young democracy, as radicalised student leaders organised strikes and violent demonstrations which would last for three years and seriously hamper formal education for a whole generation of young Malians.

For three years, three successive governments and three Prime Ministers failed to resolve the crisis. President Konaré, although politically naive and perceived to be weak, did at least dare to rely on a democratic and political process, rather than using the army to defeat the dissident students. But in the end his third Prime Minister, Ibrahim Keita, arrested the student leaders for airing a call to arms on a local radio programme.

These events were crucial to Mali, for the simple reason that the experiment in democracy survived. It became very evident during those troubled months that no one in Mali knew exactly how a democracy should function. While the constitution is largely based on the French model, the American, Canadian, Dutch, and German models are also being promoted through training and exchange programmes funded by these nations. If democracies are forever evolving, and if democratic values take generations to become part of any society's fabric, Mali is in dire need of creating its own brand of democracy. To do so, it will need not only visionary leadership but — more importantly — the active participation of each and every Malian citizen. And while the politicians and student leaders were battling it out in Bamako, the silent majority of Malians, and the poorest among them, were testing these new freedoms and quite possibly inventing Malian democracy along the way.

The Sabalibougou test case

Sabalibougou is one of the biggest *quartiers* in the ever-spreading suburbs of Bamako. This poor area was recently the site of a significant campaign by ordinary people to claim their rights under the law. Daba Coulibaly, the leader of a Malian non-government organisation called Stop-Sahel, and himself a resident of Sabalibougou, explains:

'Not so long ago this area was all fields. People came and settled here from the

James Hawkins/Oxfam

countryside after the droughts of the 1970s and 1980s. Then a new road was built through our *quartier*, to link the city centre with the airport. It was a prestige development, and the authorities planned to allocate plots of this now prime land along the road to speculators, who would sell it off to rich people. There was a plan for streets, market areas, and public spaces, but this meant that many poor people would have had to move out of their homes to make way for these new developments.

'In September 1993 we were informed that the bulldozers would be coming to tear down our houses. We were told that this was not a place for poor people: as it was the entrance to the city, new and

above Sabalibougou: 'Our biggest problem is water. There is no mains service, and the public well is dry. We have to buy all our water from street vendors. It costs 250 CFA for 60 litres — and twice that on public holidays.'

above Enterprise and resourcefulness on the streets of Bamako: Bassi Konaré sells pails made from old tomato tins

beautiful housing was needed; and, as poor people didn't have beautiful homes to show, they had to leave.

'Those of us who knew how to read and write, who were considered intellectuals by the other people, started up an association — the Association of Residents of Eastern Sabalibougou — to fight this. The aim was to rehabilitate this sector and to set up economic and social projects for the well-being of the people of the area.

'We adopted rules and set subscription fees, and from then on every Sunday we had meetings with all the members. We proceeded to hire two law firms, and deposited a complaint at the Supreme

Court. In August 1994 the Supreme Court ruled in our favour. The judgement annulled the demolition order; it said that roads and public places were to be provided, but that all development had to be done in consultation with the population and with regard to their collective interest.

'This was the first case of its kind and established a vital precedent. Many members of the Bamako elite told us: "You can't fight this. In Mali the Constitution decrees that the government owns all land." By winning our case, we have proved that ordinary citizens can fight the government and win. Now they know that if ordinary citizens organise, and they have the law on their side, they are a force to be reckoned with.

'But the people have to be vigilant and wary of the authorities. They must follow the law step by step. The battle goes on!'

That such a case was brought to court by a group of citizens and that they were able to win is testimony to the changes that are taking place within Malian society.

Giving poor people a voice

The arrival of democracy has also brought some important changes in the way that local NGOs (non-government organisations) work with poor communities.

While Malian institutions and the constitution have changed, the individuals who exercise power in the towns and countryside have not necessarily changed their ways of working. Moreover, the people whose lives they affect have not been informed about the way that democracy functions, and about the rights and obligations of the citizenry. How can people be trained in such an abstract subject, in a country where communications are difficult at best, where 80 per cent of the population is illiterate, and communities are isolated within a vast territory?

The Near East Foundation (NEF) is a US-funded NGO that has been working in

Mali since 1983. By decentralising decision-making powers and financial resources to its Malian staff, this international NGO has become in fact a Malian NGO, employing over 50 people, all Malians, in the remote Douentza area, in the Mopti region.

The Mopti region is a fascinating area, a microcosm of the nation with all the livelihoods and all the cultural groups present. The Niger and Bani rivers meet in the city of Mopti to form the vast, meandering Niger Delta. The Delta, with its annual floods, was once prosperous and still has enormous potential, with its fishing grounds, rice paddies, and huge herds of cattle and sheep, attracted to the excellent grazing land along the river banks and the lakes that form in the rainy season. But it would not be a microcosm of Mali if it did not also contain the hot and arid Douentza region.

The Douentza Circle (an administrative sub-division of Mopti) covers over 18,000 square kilometres, and has an estimated population of 168,000, consisting of Peulh (Fulani), Songhay, Dogon, Bambara, and Touareg groups, among whom the Peulh are the largest. Many young and able-bodied people migrate to Bamako and elsewhere, because the local economy, based on agriculture, herding, and commerce, is in decline. Poor rainfall leads to poor soil, which increases the competition between farmers and herders for land and water: there are frequent serious conflicts between these two groups. Education and health services are few and far between. The population is poor and illiterate. People have little access to information: there are no telephones or newspapers, and — apart from the lone tarmacked national highway to Gao — the transport system is unreliable, with rough and weather-beaten tracks.

The NEF has worked in this difficult area for many years, developing a large and complex programme which includes credit schemes, water and soil conservation, and more recently support for democracy and the decentralisation of power.

above *Pirogues* — traditional fishing boats — tied up on the banks of the River Bani at Mopti

James Hawkins/Oxfam

above The Voice of Douentza: Bocoum Koumbourou Koita begins her morning broadcast to women in the Mopti region

Power to the people through a solar-powered radio

In July 1993 NEF opened a locally controlled radio station, broadcasting initially in Peuhl, and later in Dogon and Bozo, to serve isolated and vulnerable populations. It offers traditional music, played by local musicians, and interviews with local people. These are interspersed with short stories and features about local history, and brief information pieces about improved agricultural and pastoral techniques; about health, environmental matters, and market prices. The radio

station also broadcasts summaries of regional, national, and international news in local languages; and information on legal rights and changes in Malian law, especially as these relate to women. The programmes promote the decentralisation process, and aim to equip people to participate in local government.

The radio, totally solar-powered, is called Radio Daande Douentza (RDD) — the Voice of Douentza. It is controlled by a local organisation, APROCOR. RDD was an immediate success, partly because it has no competition, but also because for the first time the people of the region have gained a voice. Between July and August 1993 the number of radios in the region increased by 140 per cent. Possession of radios had long been the privilege of menfolk, but now women began the task of fattening goats for the specific purpose of selling them to raise the money to buy a radio in order to follow the programmes.

Bocoum Koumbourou Koita is in charge of programmes for women. She covers issues like health and hygiene. 'We talk about the importance of clean water to women and children. I also interview women about problems during pregnancy, and other things like nutrition, prices in the market, contraception and family planning. Unfortunately, women are very busy and it's a problem for them to find the time to listen. Some men think it is a waste of time for women to listen to the radio. We broadcast women's programmes in the morning, so that they can listen undisturbed while the men are in the fields.'

It is difficult to find hard evidence to evaluate the impact of RDD on the population, but there are signs that it has stimulated attendance at literacy classes and the provision of health services, and eased the task of administration in such a large area. However, the real test of this unique adventure in informing and training poor people will soon come with the advent of decentralisation.

Decentralisation — what does it mean?

Decentralisation is probably the most talked about and least understood reform to be undertaken in democratic Mali.

For decades, the country had been centrally managed from government offices in Bamako; and for years, people paid taxes to civil and military administrators for non-existent services. During the National Conference which followed the *coup d'état*, delegates from all walks of life demanded that Mali should decentralise its administration by giving important powers to local authorities. This reform was enshrined in the new Constitution and, since taking power, President Konaré has repeatedly made decentralisation the key means by which both democracy and development can be attained. He has appointed a Decentralisation Team, composed of experts in various fields, to draw up the legal framework for this radical reform. The Team developed a national programme of information and training, designed to prepare for local elections in 1996 — the next phase of the massive decentralisation process.

There is widespread enthusiasm for decentralisation, but there are fears, too. There are obvious risks in delegating powers and resources to small local governing bodies in a country with an illiteracy rate of 80 per cent. There is a fear that redefining the boundaries of these local authorities will reopen the cultural and ethnic question and weaken the national Malian identity. In a country with a multitude of ethnic and cultural groups and ancient boundaries, the new local structures could mark a return to government along ethnic lines. These and other fears are real and understandable.

The advocates of decentralisation reply that Mali has not much to lose, and much to gain, by bringing power closer to the people. They argue that the reforms will give wide powers to locally elected representatives, who will rely on professional administrators to help them to implement their policies. They point out that Mali has a long history of solving ethnic tensions without resorting to violence; and that when traditional conciliation methods did break down, the previous centralised forms of government could not prevent groups like the Touaregs from fostering resentment that led to rebellion.

The greatest discontent is expressed, of course, by those who have most to lose by the reforms: the ruling class of administrators who have wielded enormous power in Mali since Independence. They are more feared than respected, and do not look forward to the day when their former subjects will be giving them orders and taking decisions for them to implement.

NGOs and civil society

National non-government organisations (NGOs) are a relatively new phenomenon in Mali. Until the advent of democracy they were barely tolerated by the authorities; but then their number increased from fewer than 100 to more than 600 in just four years. Many of them exist on paper alone: they were established merely to create work for young urban graduates, with no development experience, who before the cutbacks in government spending would have found automatic employment in the civil service. But credible and dedicated Malians are active in a growing number of Malian NGOs which, with support from external funders, are building strong links with their community base, and developing democratic internal procedures.

In recent years, many of these more dynamic NGOs have moved out of the capital city to work in more isolated regions. They specialise in fields such as soil and water conservation, credit and savings, women's issues, or urban work.

But in such a poor country, with a tiny and impoverished middle-class, Malian NGOs are entirely dependent on external donors for their funds.

With the advent of decentralisation, these versatile and flexible structures may be called to play an important role in developing local expertise and investing in local development projects.

Walde Kelka: whose wood is it anyway?

The Kelka zone in the Douentza Circle of the Mopti region of north-central Mali is an arid land, with poor rainfall, poor soils, and widespread poverty. Farming can't support a family without extra income from other sources. There is a market for fuel-wood in the city of Mopti, so many farmers add to their incomes by gathering wood in the forest.

By Malian law, land and resources belong to the State, and permission to cut wood has to be granted by the local authorities. But this does not mean that forests are managed effectively. In the words of local farmer Nouhoum Coulibaly: 'Anyone could go to Mopti and get an official paper and come into our area and cut down wood. We watched helplessly as outsiders took our wood, and there was nothing we could do about it.'

In 1992, local villagers, supported by NEF, the Malian NGO whose work has already been noted, held a meeting to discuss ways of managing their own natural resources. Thirteen villages agreed to set up an association called *Walde Kelka*. Its constitution gives local people the right to regulate the exploitation of their lands. They drew up rules concerning the collection of green and dead woods. They redefined some of the paths used by migrating groups, in order to conserve dry-season pastures. With the agreement of the local Forestry Commissioner, outsiders are no longer

below Firewood for sale in Tonka market

Jeremy Hartley/Oxfam

allowed to cut wood in the area. The Association resolves conflicts between the member villages, and between the member villages and others outside the forest area.

Walde Kelka also encourages its members to invest in the development of their area. Maouloua Dicka, Chair of the Association for Amba village, explains: 'NEF advised us on the marketing of our wood: for example, to fix the price at 55CFA per bundle, rather than 50CFA, so we could put the extra five francs into the common fund. We've really seen the benefits of this. The fund is there if we need a pump in the village, or to welcome guests. If you have to borrow money, you are more at ease when you borrow from an organisation, where the terms are clear, rather than borrowing from an individual.'

Moussa Minta, a councillor in Amba village, says: 'What I like about the Association is that there is agreement. It's very good to see 13 villages pulling together in the same direction. This has never happened before. ... All the villagers are members of the Association. If a meeting is convened, everybody comes, even the children.'

This pioneering scheme is a practical example of the sort of local democratic power structure which should emerge all over Mali as the national decentralisation process gathers pace.

top right A credit agent for the Popular Bank in Takouti Village, Douentza Circle, watches a local NGO accountant counting the money collected from members

bottom right Volunteer committee members of the Kokolo Village Bank, on the Dogon Plateau

James Hawkins/Oxfam

James Hawkins/Oxfam

Peace and reconciliation

right Touareg nomads tend to be suspicious of outsiders and government authorities

The northern conflict

Since the destruction of the trans-Saharan salt trade by the French colonialists in the early 1900s, the nomadic Touareg people have felt their very existence threatened. They had always had an uneasy relationship with any external and centralising force, and during the first world war they rebelled when the French authorities tried to requisition their camel herds for the war effort. This rebellion was harshly repressed, as was their challenge to the Malian authorities in 1963, when the newly independent government, having failed to consult them when defining the political boundaries of the new nation, restricted their right to cross borders into neighbouring countries.

In June 1990, an armed group attacked government offices in the town of Menaka. This prompted a Sahara-wide uprising of Touaregs living in parts of Mali, Niger, and Mauritania — their traditional nomadic territory of Azaouad, which they aspired to turn into an independent Touareg State.

The rebel forces were highly mobile, well trained, and equipped with sophisticated weaponry by Colonel Khaddafi of Libya. Many were the descendants of the 1963 rebels who had fled from Mali after their defeat; growing up in Libya, they had fought as mercenaries in the Western Sahara conflict against Morocco in the 1980s.

The objectives of the rebels were complex. They were not merely seeking revenge on the Malian authorities: they also attacked traditional Touareg leaders who had grown rich and powerful during the famine years by controlling most of the food aid that flooded the north. They declared an end to the continued slavery of the black-skinned Bella people, traditionally subservient to the Touareg. They denounced the economic marginalisation of the north, whose needs had been almost totally ignored by central government in Bamako.

The rebellion touched a raw nerve not only throughout the north with the Songhay, Peuhl (Fulani), and Bozo majority, but also across most of rural Mali, which had similarly been neglected by the government. The corrupt Malian army could not match the well-equipped rebels; the government was internally weakened by the nascent democratisation movement; within weeks, Moussa Traoré was negotiating for peace.

The failure of the first peace talks

The *Acords de Tamanrasset*, signed in January 1991, brought no reprieve for the Traoré regime. The Songhay and Peuhl populations in the north resented the special status conferred on the Touaregs by the proposal for a quasi-independent Touareg territory with highly de-centralised powers. This controversy was overtaken in March 1991 by the civil unrest in Bamako in March 1991, which led to the *coup d'état* led by Colonel Touré.

Touré's transitional government signified its intention to respect the peace accords, but the leaders of the Touareg rebels saw an opportunity to maximise their gains, and continued to attack government and military targets — and also civilian sites. The Malian army retaliated harshly with attacks against civilian nomadic sites. The cycle of violence was broken by the arrival of French, Mauritanian, and Algerian negotiators, who brought about an agreement known as the *Pacte National* in April 1992.

... and the failure of the Pacte National

The new agreement made significant concessions to the northern rebels, including pledges of investment in the infrastructure and economy of the region, and a commitment to decentralise important government powers to enable local communities to administer their own affairs. Although the official rebel leaders and President Konaré, elected in June 1992, were committed to the peace process, and although key elements of the *Pacte* were soon implemented, the situation gradually got worse, not better, and the country was soon on the brink of a full-scale civil war.

One reason for the impending tragedy was the fact that the Touareg have never been a unified entity, as they are sometimes falsely depicted by the international media. They are a grouping of factions, each with its own territory and internal social structures. The fragile equilibrium of Touareg society, already severely damaged by the droughts of the 1970s and 1980s, was shattered by the rebellion of the 1990s. In the resulting power vacuum, the leadership was contested by at least half a dozen armed factions. Together with their allies, the 'Arab' population of the north (white-skinned people of Moorish ancestry), many of the warlords were Malian in name only, having been raised outside the country, with no understanding of the social structure of the region.

Armed banditry was a continuing problem. The rebel leaders failed to control their former fighters who had supposedly been demobilised; the Army failed to control the former rebels who had been integrated into its ranks. Men bearing Kalashnikovs strolled openly in Gao and other northern towns, terrorising the local people, and plundering the stores of non-government organisations.

Another reason for the failure of the peace process was the question of refugees: between 100,000 and 250,000 of them, living in camps in Algeria,

above Touareg refugees from the conflict in the north

Mauritania, and Burkina Faso. In addition, tens of thousands of Touaregs and Malian Moors were displaced internally within Mali, in flight from attacks by their former neighbours, the Songhay and Peulh. Their homes had been pillaged, their belongings lost, their family members killed, and their herds stolen. For any kind of long-term peace to be established, these populations had to return home; but the widespread instability in the north did not encourage them to risk returning.

'Mobs went on the rampage in Gao, attacking and looting Touareg homes. My own house was attacked several times, and it was only the intervention of my neighbours — both Touareg and Songhay — that stopped the mob taking all my possessions. With all that has happened in the last five years, I really should be dead. Once the Touareg rebels appeared at my family's compound and claimed that I was part of Ganda Koy, the Songhay militia. At the same time as they were threatening to kill me, I found that my name was on the death list of the Ganda Koy.'
(Abou Ag Assibit)

The third reason for the breakdown of the peace process was the perceived weakness and indecision of President Konaré. He allowed the peace commission, based in Bamako, to become bogged down in bureaucratic considerations. Ordinary people in the north had no access to the talks, which soon became dominated by endless annexes and memoranda attached to the text of the *Pacte*, as the rebels demanded — and got — significant concessions from the State. Hundreds of jobs in the civil service and the army were being given away to the rebels, while structural adjustment programmes deprived most other Malians of any government employment.

The conflict spreads

By 1994, any political or popular support for the peace process had been forfeited. The situation in northern Mali was so tense that the Songhay population decided it was time to act. The largest cultural group in the north, with many influential members in the army and the government, announced the creation of a militia, called Ganda Koy. Claiming that the government backed this militia, the rebel representative on the peace commission quit and joined a new Touareg rebel force to challenge Ganda Koy. The latter won the first battle; retaliations followed, and many atrocities were inflicted on peaceful Songhay and Touareg communities.

Inevitably the population of the whole country became polarised by the conflict. There were pogroms against 'white-skinned' Malians in almost every town and city. European and North American embassies and project staff were targeted as alleged supporters of the Touareg rebel cause; even Malian NGOs were attacked, as recipients of funds from international agencies. The international bodies which could have played a reconciling role were themselves branded as pro-rebel by their own ill-advised and misinformed diagnosis of the situation. The international media, the French in particular, oversimplified the issues, portraying the Touareg rebels as exotic and romantic figures on camels, the innocent victims of the 'villains' of the piece: the southern and black Malians.

Cool heads were needed in this crisis, but the voices of moderation were silenced. Moderates were seen as either weak or as traitors to their country. Then the Malian army stepped in.

After the 1991 coup, both Colonel Touré, the transitional Head of State, and Konaré, the new President, had wanted to destabilise the army, in order to discourage any attempt at a military *coup d'état*. This had further demoralised an already undisciplined army, especially among the badly paid non-commissioned officers (NCOs). Konaré, unable to bring peace between the warring Touareg and Songhay militias, sent in the army. But the NCOs refused to obey orders and set out to impose their own brand of peace, by taking sides in the conflict.

The crisis intensified when the military executed a Swiss diplomat who was touring the Timbuktu region. In late October 1994, when the Touaregs launched their most spectacular offensive by attacking the military stronghold of Gao, the military refused to defend the city or its inhabitants. Instead, when the killings were over, they attacked a peaceful Touareg nomadic community on the outskirts of Gao, brutally killing over 200 civilians.

Turning the tide of violence

Mali was on the brink of civil war. Its international reputation was in tatters, as a campaign of disinformation accused the government of genocide. News of the latest military massacre left southern Malians in a state of shock and disbelief. The social fabric woven during centuries of sharing a common land and identity was unravelling. Many people doubted that it could be mended. But they misunderstood the essential spirit of Mali.

'We are all victims of this conflict. Everybody has been hurt in some way. Members of my family lost all their possessions. I lost some very good Touareg friends. Worst of all, I lost a sister-in-law. She was pregnant, and travelling to Gao by boat because the road wasn't safe. There had been a rebel raid somewhere nearby and in retaliation the Songhay militia attacked the boat. Although she was a Songhay, she had very fair skin, and they killed her because they thought she was a Touareg. It just shows the futility of the fighting. It had to stop.'
(Sada Maiga)

'When farmers and nomads came together to discuss the situation, they realised that they have much more in common than they have dividing them. They need each other; they have lived together in a complementary way for centuries. Ordinary people are tired of violence; they have really suffered, physically and economically, from the havoc.'
(Ibrahim Ag Idbaltanat)

above Peace makers: from left to right, Abou Ag Assibit, Sada Maiga, and Ibrahim Ag Idbaltanat, who made the first move to bring warring factions together for peace talks in 1994

In November and December 1994, several individuals, Touareg and Songhay, all working for international and local NGOs in the north, united in solidarity with the voiceless and impoverished Touareg and Songhay communities in the region. This singular act of courage set in motion a series of meetings between the communities, in an effort to break their isolation and heal the pain and distrust inflicted during five years of conflict.

After months of this process, from December 1994 to July 1995, a fragile peace had come to northern Mali. Communities had asked each other's forgiveness; armed combatants had given up their weapons; banditry had receded; and plans had been drawn up by funders and the government for an economic development programme for the north. This culminated in a formal meeting of the former warring parties and represent- atives of all northern communities, who signed a peace pact which this time was focused on local development for the

benefit of all groups. The armed Touareg umbrella group, the MFUA (Mouvement des fronts unis de l'Azaouad) announced its own dissolution.

This process culminated in March 1996 with the ceremonial burning of 3,000 weapons, surrendered by demobilised fighters, in Timbuktu, in the presence of President Konaré and representatives of all the warring parties. There was only one element in the process which all other attempts at reconciliation had lacked: control by the communities themselves.

Arbon Kama Maiga, Chair of the Mon- itoring Committee, observes: 'What is new is that the social fabric has been torn apart, and the work of the Peace Commiss- ion has been to knit society together again. One of the cornerstones of this approach is that the leaders of each community continue to meet. We are recreating our traditional ways, and that inspires us for the future. It's not new. People are bound to live together side by side. God has given them the same land to live on.'

Sustainable development

The economy

Despite the structural adjustment programmes adopted in the early 1980s and
despite the radical political reforms of the
1990s, Mali remains one of the poorest
countries in the world. In 1993 its Gross
Domestic Product equalled just 0.2 per
cent of the GDP of France, the former
colonial power. This vast, landlocked area
in the middle of the Sahel, with its fragile
soils and low rainfall and lack of infrastructure, depends almost totally for its
export earnings on agriculture and livestock herding. Against all the odds, in the
last ten years Mali has actually become
self-sufficient in cereal production and
produces very nearly all the rice that it
consumes.

The industrial and manufacturing
sector is virtually confined to Bamako.
Still reeling from the damage done during
riots of 1991 and the pillaging of 1994, it
produces only a negligible proportion of
the country's needs — about 15 per cent
of GDP.

Buried treasure

Nobody can put a value on the potential
contribution that could be made by minerals and precious metals to the economy
of Mali. In theory, it could be very considerable. For hundreds of years, gold and
diamonds have been mined on a small
scale in the south and west of the country.
The French neglected the mining sector,
and the post-Independence para-statal

left A truck leaving
Tonka market. Poor
roads and a lack of
public transport
services hold back
the development of
Mali's economy

Jeremy Hartley/Oxfam

mining company was corrupt and inefficient. Now, however, the government is taking measures to encourage foreign investment, and companies based in the USA, South Africa, and Australia are beginning to exploit the remote area south of Kayes, which is potentially very productive, but completely cut off from the capital city except for the dilapidated rail line from Dakar to Bamako.

Another constraint on the mining industry is the problem of energy supplies. At present, over 90 per cent of national energy needs are met from fuelwood and charcoal (which leads, of course, to severe deforestation). However the Manantali Dam on the Senegal River is expected to start generating hydro-powered electricity in 1998, and this should give a vital boost to the mining sector.

Beside gold and diamonds, there are deposits of bauxite, manganese, zinc, copper, and lithium waiting to be surveyed and extracted. But this is all in the future. At present, the economy of Mali is dangerously dependent for foreign exchange on the production and export of one main commodity: cotton.

Cotton: the white gold of Mali

Malians refer to cotton as 'white gold'. The cotton they grow is of high quality, and in the last ten years Mali has become the largest producer in West Africa. The harvest in 1995 was 400,000 tons — compared with 272,000 tons only four years previously. But this success has brought mixed blessings. To start with, its dependence on cotton leaves the national economy vulnerable to fluctuations in world prices: Mali was very hard hit by the fall in world cotton prices in the late 1980s and early 1990s. Nevertheless, Mali has doubled and trebled the land area dedicated to cotton, especially in the south, where rainfall and soils are better. Thus an ever larger number of farmers are at the mercy of international markets.

Mali could earn more from its cotton if it could find ways of adding value to its crops of raw cotton by processing it. At present, 98 per cent of the cotton crop is exported in unprocessed form. But there is a strong demand abroad for the typical *bogolan* motifs (designed by the late Chris Seydou, based on traditional mud-cloth patterns), and the potential for developing the textiles industry, given

below Moro Boré, a farmer in Bougouitie, Douentza Circle, in his cotton field. He also grows rice and sorghum.

James Hawkins/Oxfam

suitable levels of investment, is very considerable.

The Malian para-statal company that manages national cotton production, the Compagnie Malienne d'Industrie du Textile (CMDT), has managed to make substantial reductions in its costs and bureaucracy, and all price controls have been abolished. The CMDT works with the peasant producers, encouraging them to create village associations, and offering training in literacy and financial management. Its advice to smallholders to intercrop cotton with cereals and cash crops such as groundnuts and soya beans has proved very successful.

After the arrival of democracy, Malian cotton farmers created producers' trade unions, which now negotiate with the CMDT on everything from producer prices to quality control, from fertiliser stocking to prices. These unions should, in the future, be a force to be reckoned with in rural Mali.

Rice production

Mali is almost self-sufficient in rice, but has hardly begun to tap the enormous potential of the Niger River Delta. Only 5,000 hectares of land produce rice, while in theory about one million hectares are available for irrigated farming.

Most of the rice is grown in the area of the Office du Niger (ON), north of the city of Ségou in what was once the highly ambitious but ill-fated attempt by colonial France to exploit the river's flood levels to make this the Nile of West Africa.

The ON has been drastically restructured in recent years, trimming down its bloated bureaucracy to the bare minimum, and empowering the producers who live along the irrigation canals. Previously abandoned land is back in production; the dilapidated irrigation network is being repaired; and yields of rice are improving. Farmers have been encouraged to form and manage marketing units which gradually

Jeremy Hartley/Oxfam

developed into a sort of producers' union. Its representatives negotiate with ON officials on everything from controlling water levels in the canals to the choice of rice varieties and target production levels.

above Near Timbuktu: a farmer irrigates his rice field, using the traditional bowl-and-rope system

Livestock

Large proportions of the Malian herds of cows, sheep, and goats died in the drought of 1984. But since then the biggest herds in West Africa have reconstituted themselves and are once again making an important contribution to the country's export earnings. One problem is that local meat prices and export revenues are vulnerable to the impact of cheap imports from overseas, such as frozen beef from Argentina, and the heavily subsidised, low-quality beef which was dumped in West Africa by European nations in the late 1980s and early 1990s. Another problem is the lack of refrigeration facilities and the poor roads, which make bulk transport of carcases almost impossible.

The devaluation of the CFA Franc in 1994, the first in a series announced for the future, did produce greater revenues for exported livestock and rice. While everyone is still waiting for the dust to settle on this controversial devaluation, which affected the whole of former French Africa, the demand for cheaper Malian meat did give a bonus to Malian herders. In the cotton industry, however, the rise in

right A livestock
market at Tonka,
near Goundam

the cost of imported fertiliser and
machinery was transferred to the
producers, who will not necessarily
benefit from increased world prices.

Cereals

The production and marketing of cereals
(mainly millet, sorghum, and maize) have
benefited from major reforms that started
in the mid-1980s, when markets were
liberalised and producer and consumer
price controls were abolished. Generally,
this restructuring can claim to have had a
positive effect in the southern rural areas,
by favouring cereal production at the
expense of the mighty cotton, by
providing marketing credit funds to
village associations, and by improving
cereal distribution to most regions.
Unfortunately, the reforms have not
reached the poorer and more isolated
communities in the Sahelian zones, which
still lack proper distribution facilities and
village institutions such as cereal banks.

Farmers organise in Koro

Agriculteurs Sans Frontières (ASF) is a
local association set up in 1992 in the Koro
area of Mopti Region, in north-central
Mali. Koro is the cereal-producing zone in
the otherwise arid and drought-prone
region of Mali. Most of the inhabitants are
Dogons who came down from the
Bandiagara Cliffs and Plateau in search of
a better life in the Koro plains.

While the land is relatively rich, the
water table is desperately low, and
locating and digging wells is a daunting
task for local people, who have to dig by
hand in hard rock to depths of 80 metres
(240 feet) or more. Ever-increasing
demand for farming land means that
woodland areas are dwindling, and it is
common to see village women using
millet stalks for fuel, thus depriving the
fields and the livestock of rich nutrients
from the stalks, which should be left to rot
into the soil. Another problem is
transport. As in many other regions of this
vast country, the roads are poorly
maintained and farmers can't get their
produce to market. This leaves them at the

mercy of middlemen, who come into the area and buy up crops at knock-down prices.

The ASF was created by local people who knew they could not count on the government any more, and also realised that they could not wait for the arrival of an NGO to help to solve their problems. More and more of their young men were leaving the area to find work elsewhere, because cereal crops were not profitable. Many of these young men sought jobs in the plantations of Côte d'Ivoire, and many were returning only to die from AIDS, contracted in Abidjan, the capital, where the disease is rife.

The ASF works mainly in a group of six Dogon villages around the city of Koro, but has a loose link with a network of 80 more. It is entirely controlled by peasant members from local communities. Only one member is fully literate, but the creators of ASF are visionaries, who see their small association one day becoming a federation of villages in the Koro area. Their self-help philosophy is summed up by Jean Podiougou, the General Secretary, and Yatouna, a mother from Kiri village.

Jean: 'One of our many problems is how to get a nurse to come and treat our sick children. The health centre is 40 km away, so we have appointed our own village health workers. We chose volunteers from the villages to go to be trained by government health trainers.'

Yatouna: 'We women buy sheep; an NGO gave us the money for the first lot. We fatten them with leaves and pounded millet, and then about eight months later we sell them. But we had to pay for a vet to keep the animals healthy. Instead of calling a vet from Koro every time, we sent three people for paravet training, so they could look after the sheep in our village. This is much more economical for us.'

Jean explains how the Association is trying to beat the middlemen who exploit the farmers of this remote area: 'We have a common field. We work it communally

and the produce is held in common. In years when the harvest is bad, we use this produce to put in the cereal bank. We sell it to villagers at a price they can afford, which stops them having to go outside to buy seed from traders who profit from our misfortune.'

above Agona Bamadio, a farmer who represents his village of Gnini at meetings of Agriculteurs Sans Frontières

Beverley McAinsh/Oxfam

41

Molibemo — 'Let's Stick Together'

James Hawkins/Oxfam

James Hawkins/Oxfam

The people of the Plateau

In a country which has one of the hottest climates on earth (averaging between 40 and 48 degrees Celsius — 105–120 °F — in the last months of the dry season), the Bandiagara Plateau is reputed to be hotter than anywhere else. This is due to the fact that the whole Plateau is literally a bed-rock, with practically no top-soil, few trees, and a few dry river-beds here and there. This inhospitable land has been the home of the Dogon people for several centuries, since the time when they fled from the advance of Islam.

Dogon villages, whether on a cliff, a plateau, or a plain, have a very distinctive appearance. They are crowded with mud-built granaries, with millet-stalk thatched roofs shaped like witches' hats. Most Dogon men are polygamous, and each wife acquires her own granary at the birth of her first child. Most villages have a small mud mosque, an equally small church, and a discreet altar for animistic ceremonies. Each village also has a *togouna*: an open-sided meeting place where the men come to discuss and settle disputes. The ceiling is only high enough to allow people to sit down — the idea being that they cannot get up to fight over their disagreements. The *togouna* is square-shaped, like all Dogon buildings and baskets. In each village there is a house occupied only by menstruating women. Ironically, the taboo which keeps them apart from the rest of the community provides a much-needed respite in the women's arduous lives.

The Plateau was always prone to droughts, but those of the 1970s and 1980s were compounded by population pressures and environmental decline. Ever-dwindling crops forced the Dogon to leave the Plateau in droves, and today Dogon traders can be found in every Malian city and in the more prosperous south, where they have adapted their farming techniques to the more moderate and humid climate.

To do any farming on the Plateau requires not just the skill to survive in this harsh environment, but also the Dogons' stubbornness to succeed where no others could. Known as hard workers, the Dogons grow old quickly on the Plateau. Survival is a family matter, and Dogon men, women, and children labour constantly to assure each other's needs.

How to grow onions on rocks

Droughts and diminishing crops have forced the Dogons to adapt their ways. Since the 1930s they have had to develop a cash crop to supplement their meagre harvests of millet and sorghum. Over the years they have specialised in growing onions — which they discovered, by trial and error, need less soil and less water than other crops, and are easier to store. To grow onions, they have built small stone barriers in the now dry river-beds and gullies, to capture the rainwater which erodes what is left of the soil from the plateau. If there is enough water, the farmers then collect soil from where the wind and rains have carried it. It is an

facing page Ire Ly Village and a *togouna* — a traditional Dogon meeting place

below A stone barrier to catch rainwater, and a row of crops growing on a rock

impressive sight on the Plateau in the middle of the dry season, in December and January: lush green onions growing on tiny family plots, amid the arid brown landscape and reddish rocks. Children and women, and sometimes men, go back and forth from the water source to their plots, carrying on their heads huge jugs of water for the thirsty onion plants.

Once the plants have matured (there can be two onion seasons, Allah and the rainfall willing), the women pound the vegetables. They then make onion balls, which are laid out in the sun to dry. Once dry, they are sold to traders who know that the famous Dogon onions are awaited by city dwellers in Bamako, and even as far away as Ouagadougou in Burkina Faso, and Abidjan in Côte d'Ivoire.

below Samba Coulibaly selling Dogon onion balls in the Hippodrome Market, Bamako

James Hawkins/Oxfam

Beating the middlemen at their own game

But onion-growing cannot solve all the problems of the Dogon economy. The communities need a long-term solution to the complex environmental and social problems that confront them. In response to these problems, they have created a federation called Molibemo (meaning 'Let's Stick Together'). It emerged after the latest droughts, when the Bandiagara Catholic Mission needed a structure through which it could organise cereal distribution.

In 1990 Molibemo became independent of the church and started a series of activities to help the Plateau people to organise themselves. Their projects include training in literacy and financial management; developing improved techniques to conserve soil and water; creating cereal banks and, more recently, onion seed banks.

Molibemo's greatest feat has been to help farmers to beat the greedy traders who used to cheat and exploit them. For years, merchants came to the Plateau at harvest time to negotiate the purchase of onions with individual producers. As most producers could not read, write, or calculate, and the merchants owned the scales and set the prices, the farmers were at a disadvantage. Molibemo was determined to become the middleman on the Plateau. In 1991 it set the price for the entire crop, and persuaded the farmers to hold out. For the first time, the surprised merchants found themselves having to sit down and do a deal.

The victory, however, was short-lived. The following season, when negotiations failed and Molibemo tried to sell their own produce in the capital city, the merchants prevailed upon the traders to close off the Bamako market to them. The Dogons learned the hard way and lost most of their association's funds in the attempt, as the onions rotted in rented lorries outside the market.

But quitting is not a Dogon characteristic, so Molibemo decided to start a new scheme, which would at least give more independence to the producers by setting up onion seed banks, on the lines of the cereal banks which already existed.

In the past, when crops had been bad, merchants had offered loans to farmers to buy onion seeds, on the basis that they could pay them back at harvest time. Then, of course, the merchants would set the price for the onion crops, and the producers would find themselves at the mercy of the merchants, who set the prices so low that the producers could not make enough profit to keep a stock of seeds for the next season. Now each village buys seeds at the end of the dry season, and sells them to its members at reasonable rates when the sowing season begins. As well as setting up onion seed banks, the Dogon communities have established their own system of loans on 'fraternal and socially acceptable' conditions.

Another problem was the traditional method of stocking onion seeds in tightly closed granaries; this led to heavy losses when the seeds rotted. Recently, German researchers in Bandiagara have designed an improved version of the traditional granary, which should reduce the losses.

An unexpected spin-off

The consequences of community development projects cannot always be predicted. Yaya Tapili, Manager of the Onion Seed Bank in Danibomo, summarises the nutritional benefits of the scheme, but draws attention to an unforeseen social consequence too.

'Families no longer need to send their young men away to earn money to buy seeds. So there are more able-bodied people to work in the fields, and production has gone up. With the increase in production, villagers no longer need to sell off their cereal crops for cash, so we will have a secure food base for the difficult dry months.

James Hawkins/Oxfam

'As the only literate person in this village, my services were much in demand. But Molibemo has done literacy, numeracy, and management training with members of the committee, and now the work is more evenly shared.

'Socially, our village has gained in prestige, as other villages now come to sell their crops to us. Also, women come from other villages to seek marriage with men from our village.'

above Kokolo Village, Dogon Plateau: Issa Ouologuem tending saplings in a tree nursery. They will be planted near streams, to prevent soil erosion on the banks

'Our hands are like wood'

Jeremy Hartley/Oxfam

above The daily task of pounding millet in Douekire, near Timbuktu

'Our hands have been badly damaged by pounding millet. When you shake hands with a woman, it's like touching wood.'
(Hawa Dama, a mother from Kiri village)

Women's lives in Mali today

Women make up more than half of the population of Mali and they are a dynamic force in the nation's development; but their lives are still restricted in some important respects.

After independence from France, the first Malian government introduced some of the most progressive legislation in Africa concerning women's rights to inherit property, and their status within the family. Despite these liberal laws, traditional ways of life continue to define women's place in Malian society.

Since the coup of 1991, a Women's Commission, led by a government minister, has encouraged the formation of a wide variety of national, local, and urban women's groups. Unfortunately, the government's preoccupation with the 'development' of women is more cosmetic than real, and the numbers of impoverished women in the towns and countryside of Mali continue to grow.

Women in most instances play a vital role not only in the traditional sphere of the family but as providers of food and income. More and more young men are leaving home to find work and income elsewhere, and their communities are left to fend for themselves, usually under the care of women. But despite their added responsibilities, they can rarely get credit or training in new skills. Their voices are not heard, their views not taken into account, and their needs not given proper priority. They are rarely consulted by village leaders, by the government, by donors, or by NGO agents.

Women's health is imperilled by childbirth. The median age of marriage is 16, and nearly half of all Malian women are mothers by the age of 18. The maternal mortality rate is by far the highest in the world: 20 per cent of deaths among women of child-bearing age are attributed to pregnancy, which is not surprising, as only 32 per cent of births are attended by any kind of trained medical assistant, and 65 per cent of all pregnant women suffer from anaemia. The stark fact is that a woman in Mali has a one-in-seven chance of dying in childbirth or from unsafe abortion.

The statistics for girls' and women's education are equally negative, despite the present government's commitment to improving provision for them. Only 35 per cent of primary-school pupils are girls, and the proportion diminishes with every year of schooling. Only 22 per cent of girls reach a fifth year of education.

But change is slowly coming. Women are making progress through their new, if unrecognised, powers as bread winners. Unfortunately, this still translates in too many instances into an increase in their workloads and responsibilities.

Mike Goldwater/Oxfam

The Sabalibougou Credit Scheme

Sabalibougou is a sprawling area of poor housing on the edge of Bamako. It began to grow as a squatters' area in the 1980s, as people came in from the rural areas to escape the worst effects of the drought. There is no electricity in Sabalibougou, no clean water or safe sanitation system. In the rainy season, sudden sandstorms are usually the prelude to equally sudden downpours. Within minutes, the red mud tracks and yards around the tiny houses turn into fast-flowing rivers of filthy, blood-red water. Such rains come four or five times a week, and the wet season lasts for two or three months.

Many women work in the market of Sabalibougou. Their stalls, if they have

them, are flimsy creations of sticks and millet-stalk thatch, beaten tin cans, and plastic sheeting. As in most African countries, the market-place is a special focus for working women: many meet there to organise themselves and to look for opportunities for self-development.

OMAFES is a Malian NGO, working mainly in the sprawling slum areas of Bamako. It has been working in Sabalibougou since 1992, and has introduced a dynamic credit scheme, and a training programme in literacy and commercial skills which has stimulated most of the residents. At first the project was intended to benefit women; but its successes have prompted the women to argue for the inclusion of their menfolk in the credit scheme.

above Women in Mali have a one-in-seven chance of dying in childbirth or from unsafe abortion

A day in the life of Saly Fomba

'I wake up very early, about 5 o'clock in the morning. I wash, I pray, and then I go quite a distance from here to get water for the family; it takes about an hour. Then I prepare breakfast for all the family. After that, I start pounding the millet for the noon meal. After I've done the pounding, but before the meal, I go to the market to sell tomatoes, onions, and other condiments. Then I come home and finish preparing the mid-day meal.

'I was born about 150 km from here, but grew up in Bamako. But since I've been married, I've lived here in Sabalibougou: my husband is from here. I have three children, including the youngest, one-year-old Bourama. There are nine people altogether in the household, counting our relatives.

'After preparing the meal, if there's a literacy class I go to it; and then I go downtown, about 7 or 8 km from here, to buy vegetables for the next day's market.

I finish all my work around 10 o'clock at night. The main problem we have is money: how to get enough to feed and clothe our children adequately, and to pay for their health care and education.

'Things have got better in the past two years. Since the project opened here, I have received credit, which has enabled me to earn more money. Before the project, the clothes that I wore and the children wore were very shabby, but now I can buy us better-quality clothes and I can provide soap for my family.

'Before the project, I couldn't read or write; but now I can read, I can write letters, and I even fill out the forms for the reimbursements. I feel much more at ease now. Effectively I have gained in self-confidence. I feel I am much more respected, both in my family and in the community. My new skills will surely improve the lives of my children. For instance, even before they are of school age, I can try and teach them the alphabet.

below Market women in Sabalibougou, members of an OMAFES credit scheme, including Saly Fomba (standing far right) and Assitan Fomba (middle of the second row)

Beverley McAinsh/Oxfam

'I have also gained a better sense of managing larger amounts of money, because what I receive in credit far surpasses any amount I had before. And through training I have learned to play a role in the management committee and to acquire management skills.

'I received 25,000 francs (£31.00) from the project. First of all I bought a large bag of onions: onions don't perish very quickly. With the rest of the money I bought new tomatoes each day. I get by. I've always managed to repay the instalment on my loan on the day it's due.'

A household of 40 people

Assitou Fomba (no relation to Saly) has lived in Sabalibougou for 25 years. She has ten children and supports a regular household of 15-20 people, and sometimes up to 40. She comments:

'Life in Bamako these days is extremely expensive, and I have to meet all the expenses of my family. My husband hasn't got any work. Of all the women involved in the Association, none has a husband with a full-time job or a regular income. Many of our husbands came from

'There are six women in our group. Solange buys clothes and sells them in the market. Ramatou and I buy material in the central market and sell it in the Sabalibougou market. Another woman goes to Banan, which is 80 km away, and comes back the same day. She buys shea nuts, curdled milk, aubergines, and chickens, and then sells them in the local market. Fatima buys a whole truck-load of wood and sells it little by little; it can take up to 15 days. Sassetan buys vegetables from a market garden nearby.'
(Fani, leader of a women's credit group in Bamako)

the bush to find work, but they had no qualifications. Four of my ten children go to school; the others have nothing to do.

'This project is my only source of credit, so I take some of the money I make each day and use it for millet, with which I bake millet cakes to sell at the market.

'Before the credit scheme, I was having enormous problems in getting by. Now I am able to meet all the basic needs of my family — clothing, education — which otherwise would have been impossible, because my husband has no work. An added bonus is that I am now looked upon with respect, because of the role I play in the project.'

above Mamedi Keita outside his shop in N'Gol Onina Market, Bamako

A women's group that men can join

Unlike many credit schemes in Mali and elsewhere in Africa, the Sabalibougou project has successfully widened its scope to include men as well as women. In development circles, it is often said that providing credit to men is a sure way of losing the money, and that wives and children will never benefit, because the men prefer to meet some other priority. But generally, Malian men do provide for their families — if they can get work. In Bamako many women tell of fathers leaving home early in the morning to conceal their lack of work from their children.

In Sabalibougou, seeing their women benefit from the OMAFES credit scheme prompted the men to ask for membership. The women supported their request. The success of this new venture is perhaps partly due to the fact that most people in this community come from the same rural area of Mali, so a sense of loyalty to friends and neighbours has created the necessary social bonds that ensure regular repayments.

Mamedi Keita, a stallholder in N'Gol Onina Market, talks about the benefits of the OMAFES scheme: 'I'm the eldest son in my family. My father is sick, so the responsibility for meeting all the needs of my family falls on me. There is my father, who has three wives, my own immediate family, plus brothers and sisters, and altogether it comes to about 18 people.

'I like my trade very well; I have ambitions for my shop. Its name translates as "Traditions of Africa", and I would like to be able to sell traditional handcrafts from all over West Africa, not just from Mali. With the loan from OMAFES I have acquired more space to display my merchandise, and met some of my household's personal needs.

'My wife sells incense at our house. She doesn't go out to sell in the market. She wasn't eligible for the credit scheme, because she is not a member of the association. I gave her some of my credit, so she could start her own business, selling incense.'

City life

A tourist's view of Gao

Gao is the northernmost city in Mali.
Bamako, the capital, is 1,200 km away.
Gao is a place of wide sandy avenues and
open spaces. There is a traditional mud
mosque and French colonial buildings of
faded pink stucco and shady colonnades.
Most people live in square, mud houses
with roofs made concave to catch water.
On the wide green waters of the River
Niger, fishermen glide by in their graceful
boats, called *pirogues*. Along the banks,
women are washing up, scrubbing
cooking pots with sand, doing their
laundry, pounding millet. In the distance,
the distinctive huts of Fulani herders look
like up-turned baskets; close by, black and
white smudges mark where their sheep
and goats lie ruminating in the sun. A
flat-bottomed, blue metal ferry with a
noisy Italian engine and a spluttering
exhaust chugs across the river, weighed
down with trucks and carts, trinket sellers
and doughnut vendors, and jostling
livestock. Camels, sheep, and goats
scavenge in the rubbish at the side of the
roads. The whole place has a baked,
scorched feeling, and shimmers in the
heat. Citizens of Gao, both men and
women, wear vibrant, stunning colours:
flowing *boubous* of scarlet and cobalt blue,
or rich, glazed cloth of dark green or
brown. The men wear dazzling white
turbans, elaborately wound round their
heads for protection against wind and
sand; the women's scarves are fashioned
into elegant folds and peaks. They stand
out like jewels against the red-brown
backdrop of Gao.

Jeremy Hartley/Oxfam

above Pots on sale in
Tonka market

51

James Hawkins/Oxfam

above Domestic utensils made from old oil-drums and wrecked cars in a workshop near Bamako's Hippodrome Market

right A pothole in the road in Bamako

James Hawkins/Oxfam

What the tourist doesn't see

Gao is the fastest-growing city in Mali. It lacks the most basic services and infrastructure needed by a rapidly expanding population, which will soon reach 70,000. In 1960, only five per cent of Malians lived in cities. By 1990 that figure was up to 23 per cent. It is expected to reach 38 per cent by the year 2000. The population of Bamako has multiplied more than ten-fold in the last thirty years: from 76,000 in 1958 to nearly one million in 1995.

One reason for the alarming rate of urban expansion is the high birth-rate; but another, equally valid, is the constant migration from the countryside. The rural exodus has become the modern form of initiation, bringing young people into contact with other ways of living, and putting their personal strengths to the test. Life in the big cities is precarious. People's needs are more numerous and varied, and the traditional solidarity systems which used to provide for those in difficulty quickly disintegrate in an urban setting. Delinquency is on the rise in all its forms: violence, theft, drug addiction, and prostitution.

The industrial and manufacturing sector of the Malian economy is extremely weak. Without skills relevant to city life, permanent jobs are almost impossible to find. Most people try to earn a livelihood in the precarious 'informal sector' — selling anything they can get their hands on. On every street corner there are young and not so young people, selling pirated music cassettes, cigarettes, tourist trinkets, shoe-shining services, Nigerian or Taiwanese watches, and so on. It pays for the next meal, but not much more.

The lack of low-cost housing has forced thousands to the edges of the cities, where their way of life is neither urban nor rural. In Bamako, 30 per cent of the population live in peripheral shanty-towns, in cramped and insanitary housing that, being illegal, is often constructed by night. Throughout the city, only 38 per cent of homes have access to running water; 17 per cent are served by electricity; and garbage-removal services are entirely inadequate.

City life, seasonal migration, and rural exodus make for a highly mobile population of young men and women. Traditional social patterns break down, and the almost inevitable result is the spread of HIV-infection: the present rate for urban populations in Mali is 4 per cent. With an inadequate health-care system, and an almost non-existent communication strategy on AIDS prevention, there is now widespread fear that a full-blown epidemic could be on the way.

left The informal sector in action: making nails out of old oil drums in Mopti

below Hoes, ploughs, buckets, and cooking utensils made from recycled metal

James Hawkins/Oxfam

James Hawkins/Oxfam

Enterprise on the streets: instant passport photos (below), supplied to hopeful migrants like Dominie Josy Mensou (left), a barber from Ghana. Trying to work his way north towards Europe, he was refused entry into Mauritania and forced to turn back. Like hundreds of other Ghanaians, he is now trapped in Mali, lacking the money to return home.

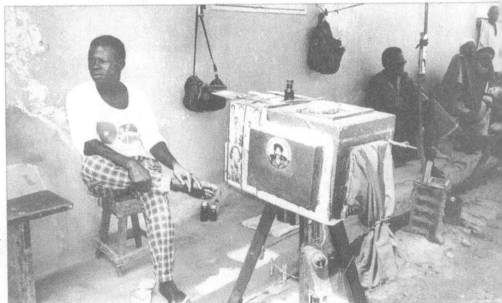

James Hawkins/Oxfam

A nation at the crossroads

During the last ten years, Malians have lived through profound and numerous changes as they tried to erase nearly a century of authoritarian rule which had defiled their very souls and their sense of honour.

Decades of colonial rule, followed by centralised mismanagement and generalised corruption, estranged ordinary Malians from those who 'governed' them. The agricultural potential of this formerly productive country suffered the pernicious consequences of drought, famine, and environmental damage. Worse still, government agents and their policies alienated the peasants and farmers with their contempt and ignorance of those who, for centuries, had accumulated expertise in the science of producing crops from the Sahel. Government administrators and politicians were just local potentates, bent on accumulating power and money at the expense of those they were supposed to serve.

In self-defence, Malians retreated to the only other source of trust and stability they knew: the traditional beliefs of the elders. But the world was changing dramatically, and soon even these old ways were being attacked from within. The oppression of women by men, and of young people by the old, were major obstacles which prevented the most dynamic and resourceful members of Malian society from playing their roles as agents of change and development. Toiling in difficult conditions, Malian women and young people were denied any autonomy, their incomes appropriated by their elders, while their voices and grievances went unheard. Stifled and frustrated, the young escaped to urban centres, where they encountered new freedoms but also misery and hardship.

Throughout the 1980s, many attempts were made to stop the country from surrendering to fatalism and unthinking submission. But they were mostly

James Hawkins/Oxfam

above A village elder in Sekolo, near Mourdiah

55

external solutions, proposed by international agencies and their teams of 'experts'. Drastic structural plans were devised by international technocrats; innumerable seminars were held to diagnose symptoms and propose solutions. But one key element remained absent from these exercises: Malians themselves.

The 1990s saw Malians take matters into their own hands. In the words of Moussa Traoré, the former dictator: *'You have to be very wary of Malians, as they are like a spring ... you can push so much, but one day that spring will bounce back and kick you in the face'*. And they did bounce back! The Touareg rebellion, the new student movement, the democratic associations, and the suicidal marches that toppled his regime were part of that 'kick in the face'. However, most of the protestors were not motivated by a thirst for democracy: theirs was a cry of despair.

What followed was no less than revolutionary, as the National Conference debated the vision of a new Mali: proposing a new constitution, establishing decentralisation as the backbone of democracy, legalising multi-party politics, drawing up a new electoral code and process, liberating the media, promoting freedom of speech and association ... This all took place in only three chaotic years, with a modicum of unrest and with respect for democratic principles.

For the huge majority of ordinary Malians — more than 70 per cent of the population — who live below the poverty line, democracy has not yet brought about any tangible and positive changes in their situation. Misery, disease, and ignorance are still the experience of too many. But for anyone who has witnessed the daily struggles of the people, both before and after the recent events, the changes are awesome. Could many countries undergo such upheavals without giving in to disorder and mass violence? Mali did, and it was able to do so because Malians had decided most of the changes, and knew that the very existence of the nation was at stake.

In towns and villages and urban ghettos, men and women, students and youth are organising, creating associations and NGOs, contributing to newspapers, participating in community projects, working on decentralisation committees, and so on. As in Koro and Sabalibougou, they are fighting the system, setting the standards of what democracy *a la Malienne* will become. The stakes are enormous, the challenge inspiring.

Yet people in the rich North rarely, if ever, hear or read about any of this through the media. When one of the poorest and most repressed countries in the world throws away its shackles, sets up democratic institutions, and tries to resolve civil conflict peacefully, this does not make headlines. When a resource-poor country ties to clean up its financial management, restructures its administration by giving powers to local communities, and encourages constitutional freedoms, the changes go unnoticed. Mali has made the right choices, but in all likelihood will have to make do with less external support from a world that seems bent on cutting aid budgets.

The hardest choices have been made. The effort required is undeniable, as even the poorer people engage in the emergence of a civil society. The problems of population growth, environmental decline, urban blight, disease, and ignorance will continue to play havoc with the hopes of all Malians. The new Mali does not have many options. The failures of the past and the challenges of the future will not be overcome without the deployment of Mali's greatest natural resource: its men and women, sons and daughters of nomads and farmers, creators of empires and designers of *cousinage*.

left A Touareg man in Gangano Village, near Bourem

Dates and events

1076–1235 Sosso Kingdom under Kanté

1235–1480s First Mali Empire

1493 Askia Mohamed founds Songhay Empire

1591 Moroccan invasion

1594 Destruction of Timbuktu University

1633 Kaarta Kingdom founded by Massassi Coulibaly

1712 Reign of Biton Coulibaly

1862 Holy *jihad* by Oumar Tall; creation of Ségou Kingdom

1880–1899 French invasion challenges Empire of Samory Touré

1900 Touré dies in captivity; Mali becomes a French territory

1960 4 April, creation of Federation of Mali with Senegal; 22 September, Federation broken; Republic of Mali proclaimed under President Modibo Keita

1968 *Coup d'état* led by Moussa Traoré

June 1990 Start of Touareg rebellion

March 1991 Mass discontent leads to military coup led by Colonel Touré and establishment of transitional government

April 1992 *Pacte National* brings temporary peace to the north

June 1992 Alpha Konaré becomes Mali's first democratically elected President

1994 Collapse of *Pacte National*; armed conflict spreads from the north to most areas of Mali

December 1994 Local NGOs in northern Mali begin the process of reconciliation.

June 1995 Peace restored.

below A young woman has her hair braided in Dili Village, north-west Mali

Mike Goldwater/Oxfam

Mali: facts and figures

Land area: 1,240,000 sq km

Population: 10.76 million (1995 estimate)

Annual population growth: 3.1 per cent

Life expectancy at birth: 46 years

Main urban centres: Bamako (pop. est. 900,000); Ségou (88,000); Sikasso (75,000); Mopti (75,000); Gao (55,000); Kayes (51,000); Koutiala (49,000)

Principal ethnic groups: Bambara, Malinké, Mandingué, Sarakolé, Bozo, Bobo, Senoufou, Peuhl, Dogon, Touareg, Songhay, Moors

Languages: Official language French (used by urban elite only); Bamanakan (dominant language of commerce) and several other national languages are widely spoken

Adult literacy: 11 per cent of women, 23 per cent of men

Primary school enrolment: 30 per cent of boys, 17 per cent of girls

Infant mortality: 161 per 1,000 live births

Maternal mortality: 850 per 100,000

Malnutrition: 31 per cent of under-fives

Vaccinations: 25 per cent of children

Access to clean water: 17 per cent of the population

Exchange rate: £1.00 = 700 CFA francs

Annual GDP per capita: US$280

GDP growth rate: 5.2 per cent (1995)

Foreign debt: US$2.8 billion (1995)

Main agricultural products: millet, sorghum, cotton, rice, livestock, peanuts

Principal exports: cotton ($156m in 1994); livestock and livestock products ($110m); gold ($62m)

Mike Goldwater/Oxfam

above Bali Village, north-west Mali, viewed from the air

Sources and further reading

Very little has been written in English about Mali, apart from highly academic studies of social and environmental topics. The present book drew on the following sources:

Le Mali, by Joseph Roger de Benoist, published by L'Harmattan, Paris (1989)

A Short History of West Africa, AD 1000 to the Present Day, by T.A. Osae, S.N. Nwabara, and A.T.O. Odunsi, published by Hill and Wang (1973)

UNDP Human Development Report, published annually by Oxford University Press

Mali: Evaluation des conditions de vie, published by the World Bank in 1993

Strategies d'assistance de la Banque Mondiale au Mali, published by the World Bank (1994)

Other relevant resources:

Adaptable Livelihoods: Coping with Food Insecurity in the Malian Sahel, by Susanna Davies, published by Macmillan (London), 1996

At the Desert's Edge: Oral Histories from the Sahel, edited by Nigel Cross and Rhiannon Barker, published by Panos/SOS Sahel (London), 1993

Changing Places? Women, Resource Management, and Migration in the Sahel, edited by Rosalind David, published by SOS Sahel (London), 1995

Living in the Sahel, an interactive video-disc about Mali, containing 25,000 photographs, 70 minutes of live sound recordings, and 20 minutes of documentary film; £10.00 from Anglia Multi-Media, Norwich NR1 3JG, UK

below Baba Dicko teaching a literacy class at Poy village

Acknowledgments

Many people contributed to the writing of this book, and I thank them all, especially Oxfam colleagues in Oxford and Bamako: Assitan Coulibaly, Yacouba Koné, Mohamed Ould Mahmoud, Catherine Robinson, Isaaka Savane, and David Waller. In particular, I thank Beverley McAinsh for her insights. Above all, I am indebted to the people of Mali for their generosity and friendship, and their inspiring daily pursuit of dignity and freedom.

Rhéal Drisdelle

right Friends in a millet field, Sekolo Village, Circle of Nara

James Hawkins/Oxfam

61

Oxfam in Mali

Most of the projects, people, and communities featured in this book are supported by Oxfam (UK and Ireland), which first became engaged in community development work in Mali in the late 1960s. The Oxfam programme expanded during the trans-Saharan drought of 1983-84, and has concentrated ever since on the more isolated and arid regions of the country. A new initiative began in 1991, with the establishment of an urban programme, based mainly in Bamako.

Oxfam's community-based development programme includes support for food-security projects; the conservation of soil and water resources; the installation of water supplies; large and small credit schemes for rural and urban women; and training in literacy and financial management skills.

In addition to these long-term programmes, working in partnership with local non-government organisations, Oxfam has been involved in the democratisation and decentralisation process, and the peace and reconciliation process in northern Mali.

To strengthen local democracy, Oxfam has supported the emergence of an independent rural radio station in the north; instituted training for Malian NGOs on democracy and decentralisation; stimulated debate by organising regional meetings between NGOs, politicians, and government administrators; and has served on a National Training Committee for the Implementation of Decentralisation.

As part of the community-based process of peace and reconciliation, Oxfam has supported the courageous network of NGOs in the north who successfully encouraged communities from both sides of the conflict to sit down together and resolve their differences. Together these communities and NGOs persuaded the combatants to lay down their arms and join them in discussing the prospects for peace and to ask for forgiveness in a joint quest for reconciliation.

below Boubacar Dicko, technician at the Oxfam-funded Radio Douentza

James Hawkins/Oxfam

left An Oxfam-funded well under construction near Timbuktu

Published by Oxfam (UK and Ireland)

© Oxfam (UK and Ireland) 1997

A catalogue record for this publication is available from the British Library.

ISBN 0 85598 334 5

Published by Oxfam (UK and Ireland), 274 Banbury Road, Oxford OX2 7DZ, UK (registered as a charity, no. 202918)

Available from the following agents:
for Canada and the USA: Humanities Press International, 165 First Avenue, Atlantic Highlands, New Jersey NJ 07716-1289, USA; tel. (908) 872 1441; fax (908) 872 0717
for southern Africa: David Philip Publishers, PO Box 23408, Claremont, Cape Town 7735, South Africa; tel. (021) 64 4136; fax (021) 64 3358.

Available in Ireland from Oxfam in Ireland, 19 Clanwilliam Terrace, Dublin 2 (tel. 01 661 8544).

Designed by Oxfam Design Department
Printed by Oxfam Print Unit

Oxfam (UK and Ireland) is a member of Oxfam International.